Status Quorum

Christian Emond

BookLeaf Publishing

India | USA | UK

Presentation by *BookLeaf Publishing*

Web: www.bookleafpub.com

E-mail: info@bookleafpub.com

ISBN: 9789357446891

First edition 2022

DEDICATION

To the curious, the passionate, the endangered, the broken hearted, and those filled with too much love. To the lost and hope to be found. Most of all to those who wonder.

For Twin #2.

ACKNOWLEDGEMENT

Allusions allow us to celebrate artists, authors, and creators that have inspired us and made a significant impact on the way we create. I would like to acknowledge some of those that have inspired me and have been given an artistic reference in this collection – Taylor Swift, Lewis Carroll, Antoine de Saint-Exupéry, Sylvia Plath, Elizabeth Bear, Roberta Williams, Ken Williams, Hidetaka Miyazaki, Sami Antero Järvi (Sam Lake), and Wisława Szymborska.

More personally I would like to give acknowledgement to those that have been immensely supportive in me pursuing my poetic endeavours. Firstly, Anika Zaman, my first fan and continual moral support, you are appreciated more than you know. From the first time I met you, I could see how compassionate and caring a person you are; if we had more Anika's in the world, peace could be possible. Second, Allison Guthrie, who has been fully encouraging and with me every step of the way in making this book. She has a beautiful heart and kind soul, not only an encyclopedia of knowledge, but a poem of a person. My sister, Jewel, who is more important than she realises to the people around her. She has made me appreciate the creative side of the world and without having her side by side with me growing up, life would be much duller. Since we were kids, I have felt most accomplished when I am able to make my sister laugh and smile.

The best parts of myself that form my quorum are my sister, mom, dad, Uncle Jason, and my late Pappy. At minimum, these are the people that I have modeled myself after; while I am not a direct mirror of any of them, I think parts of me are represented by them in everything I do.

Finally, I would like to thank everyone that has supported my first book, "Planted in Snow Soaked Grass", and who have now bought this book as well. It is an incredible feeling to think that people beyond myself or my close network have a piece of me on their shelves. I hope you enjoy the collection and thank you for reading.

PREFACE

Let it be known that I wrote with honesty and care, regardless of what you may think of my babbling Belugas.

Your first question may be about the title, "Status Quorum", and not necessarily the whales you have yet to meet, so let's unpack this. The definition of a quorum, in most senses of the word, boils down to the minimum amount of 'something A' you require to achieve 'something B', though the traditional and popular use of this term is related to members in a meeting to pass a vote of some kind, I took a generalized form. Of course, this then aligns to several use cases in relation to this collection, the writing of it, and the writer himself, me.

However, before I get into all of that, let me tell you more about the picking of the title… it did not present itself to me or my imagination for quite some time in creating this book, nor did it come expectedly. In fact, the poem that shares the book's namesake was the 15th I wrote and then struggled to provide a name for. The poem in question (Status Quorum) was written in a fit of writer's block. After having the usual frustration set in and turning to the web for potentially useful ideas or inspiration, I came across an article about Generative Pre-trained Transformer 3 (GPT-3) written by Meghan O'Gieblyn. GPT-3 is a highly advanced autoregressive language model that has been exposed to the entirety of the internet and is able to produce human-like or imitative text. Within the article, the writer talked about a number of interesting topics, mainly focused on subconscious writing and the psychology behind it. From this, came my attempt at letting go of my overactive imagination, wonderment, questioning, etc. and simply trying to write from my subconscious, to see if it had a story worth telling. The result of which, though I have yet to replicate such quality, was the poem, "Status Quorum", now a favorite of mine.

So you see, for me, Status Quorum was not only a fancy title with eloquent words, it was a way to denote the state I tried to simulate that resulted in the poem – a state of only essential brain function… or at least something like that. After writing all of the poems for the collection I was stuck to figure a title and a strong arrangement of the poems to tell an overarching story, the way I did with my first collection, "Planted in Snow Soaked Grass". In re-reading the poems over and over and reflecting on the writing, I came to realise that this collection, unlike the last, was much less about others and trying to solve an identity crisis through poetry; this collection is more mature and sure of itself, as am I. Overall, you can take this collection on some level to be the minimum amount of reading you need to do, to understand me, in this moment of time. Or perhaps this is the 'quorum' of all of the pieces of myself that make me, me. My subconscious pieces have all come together and voted on who I shall be… for now.

Before we move away from the title, another consideration that was made, comes from my background in molecular biology. I would implore you to do some looking into 'quorum sensing', it is an incredibly interesting topic. For those who are not curious enough, it generally comes down to the ability of cells to regulate their gene expression based on the cell-population around them – the pieces understand themselves in reflection of the status of others. Now if we are to take this wonderful science terminology to a place of philosophical thought, we may make the analogy at a human level to think of empathy as a sort of quorum sensing for emotions. In this way I use 'quorum' as a way to reflect that a number of the poems in this collection have been inspired by shared experiences with those around me.

My starting point for this collection was a focus on 'wonder'. Initially, I wanted to keep the collection positive and up-lifting, but as I wrote I felt it would be a dishonest reflection on myself and what 'wonder' truly is. To me, wonder is more than just bright skies, bright futures, and sighs of relief, it must also be insecurities, anxieties, and exasperation. Of course wonder, regardless of positive or negative, is often questioning. I hope to have shown a wide spectrum of wonder in this collection, after all, this book is a reflection of my own series of wonderings.

Poetry, Part I

What is a poem if not a story?
A narrative tool to evoke emotion or teach a
lesson.
Whether it be plainly written, read between
lines,
Or even rhythmically rhymed,
The poet is nothing more than a storyteller.
They write of music, muses, or things that are
amusing.
Cherry trees, strudels, or bakeries,
Drama, comedy, and tragedy,
We are simply an audience for their craft.

History has been saved in the lyrics of poets,
Culture embodied by ritualistic lines,
And here we burn their words.

Ages have been defined by the philosophy of
poems,
Kingdoms crumbled by forlorn love letters,
And incantations cast in the forges of stanzas.
Let the wonder of poetry travel across
space-time.
Teach children to express themselves,
Inform the future of our epics,

And create worlds we will never meet.
For we shall not outlive the stones we brand,
Just as the thoughts we dare not speak will die
with us,
We should seek redemption in our analysis by a
kinder generation.
To them we shall be the forefathers of mistakes,
The mothers of misfortune,
Yet we will stand as the parents of poetry.

Fall With You

There's something so beautiful about seeing the colors of fall with you.
Slowly the summer passes away and the bright, new green is stripped to reveal yellows, oranges, reds, and purples;
Tis the season for date night adventures and getting to know each other.
Patches of pumpkins will serve as a backdrop to the spice you add to my life,
With cinnamon spiked drinks in cafes, we plan our trip to the countryside.
Marigolds, asters, and dahlias bloom, opening to a cooler world with us together.
Crunching through parks with your arms around mine, we find a bench to sit and enjoy the crisp air that accompanies a setting sun on another perfect day.
Autumn tones will compliment your light green eyes, as the time passes away,
We will think back to when we fell for each other under falling stars.
Walking through the night aimless and carefree, as Polaris guided us home.

As the season gets away from us, the bright
colors of fading trees over the hill turn to white.
Homes pump clouds of smoke from their
chimneys and we cover ourselves with
increasingly cozy apparel.
We don knitted gloves and crocheted hats for
walks by the frozen lake.
The snow covered environment hushes the
sounds of the city, leaving us alone in
wonderland.
Under a park lamp I'll pull down your scarf and
kiss your rosy cheeks, hiding your blush.
With skates on and stumbling on the ice, it will
be fun to fall with you.
We will spend enough time out in the snow to
question if we have toes anymore,
But we will warm up with hot chocolate and the
mint you grew, while we decorate gingerbread
kids.
Later we will slow dance to the Bleachers and
'Lover' under string lights in your living room.
Before we kiss goodnight and the season ends, I
will let you know that,

"I could be suspended in this season with you
forever,
And forever fall with you."

Wandering Wonderer

Wander as I may, I do wonder.
I wonder what it is that has allowed me to be
here in this present of a day,
Hugged by the forest and warmed by your
pleasant company.
I have certainly wandered quite a ways away
from where I began,
From the womb with my sister to the sky with
you,
Yet to think we have not truly travelled far at all.
We have only crossed the world, whereas a
select few have crossed the thermosphere.
It really does make me wonder if we too could
one day travel where others have not, or at least
travel where we have not.
Will we reach all of our destinations in time?
And does it really matter if we were to schedule
ourselves to a location?
I certainly do feel I have journeyed, even if I did
not know where to,
I have found myself in a few places that were
new with you.

Though it does still nag me, this feeling of
answers left undiscovered,
I think I might find answers along a path that I
may rightly wander.

In this life, I have found so many questions to
wonder about, that it makes me question
whether ignorance really is bliss,
Or does it simply mean you have lost the desire
to dream up a reality where we might expand
our imagination.
Regardless, I think I may be more comfortable
perpetually questioning.
If I die before I learn my own nature, I will be
happy to join nature in its circularity,
Though if I was to find my niche in life, I only
wish that it may be open to interpretation.
For if we are to see the universe as limitless,
then let us never stop filling it with new realities.
After all, in this nearly insignificant amount of
time, I have certainly found a few things to be
significant in mine,
And I do think it is pretty wonderful that in an
infinite number of choices, mine have led to
you, and yours to me.
So may I always wonder, so that I may continue
to wander through life, with you.

To Alice

Let's go home to the woods.
Take my hand and lead me into the folklore you
have created.
Like Alice I shall willingly fall down a rabbit
hole into your life, thinking to myself, "curioser
and curioser".
I will educate myself in tea time traditions and
staying up to kiss the stars goodnight.
We can begin in the fall and build a home from
that which has died.
Cedar trees will safely hold in our warmth
against cold winter nights,
While we are wrapped around each other like a
warm august night.
We can explore the lyrics of the winter air and
create our own wonderland.
The willows would weep for the sorrows we
brought from the city,
But soon we will forget we had a life there at all.
Guided home by the fireflies that illuminate our
front porch,
We bring home vegetables and herbs for a
fantastical soup.
Through the glade we will dance like leaves
exiled from their home,

Newly discovering themselves among the
expanse of the rolling hills.

Over the years our cardigans will become worn
and mended over until they are hardly
recognizable.
When we are older and wiser, we can sing to
each other in the moonlight, finally
understanding the meaning of the music.

In the end you will wear a crown of flowers and
I will pass away into your emerald eyes,
Wondering what I had done to deserve such
peace.

Through the Hills

Rolling hills keep me alive.
For when I have spun down to the depths of a
valley at the speed of sadness,
I will rise once again over another hill basked in
the light of brilliant stars.
Sometimes I fly so high the sun itself scorches
me, as if I myself were Icarus and my wings
were never truly destined for such great heights.
Naturally I fall, a victim of my own hubris, into
the arms of rose bushes.
Beautifully bloomed in the form of a soft bed, I
embrace their thorns.
Undisturbed by my losses, the roses turn cold
and wintery to the touch,
Leading me to begin a journey to find a new
home.

Traveling the hills can become quite lonely in
the quiet of a broken heart.
Walking without path, pattern, or plans, has
often led to lost souls…
Or so I was told by my frosty friends.
Perhaps that was merely a ploy to keep me
around, so the vampiric flowers I loved so much
could continue to feast.

Far and away from where I fell, I would become
livelier, and even befriend intelligent foxes,
Companions to which I found my way through
the forest and mountain pass.

Covered by burs, my past holds tightly to my
clothes and skin,
Staying there until I stop to take the time to
distance myself from their hooks.
The glow of the iridescent skies illuminate my
scars and heal my wounds,
Allowing for a certain self-reflection on how far
I have traveled.
I look across the sprawling landscape of where I
can choose to head next,
And come to realise I may wander forever
among these hills,
But I will always be responsible for my own life.

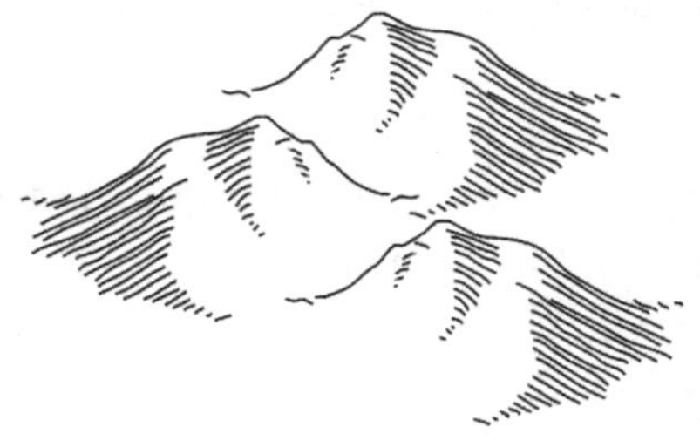

Among the Stars

Let the stars be my home for the night, for I
have nowhere else to go.
I have searched unfeeling voids for millennia,
conserving myself for some large purpose I may
never find;
Such is the life of a pilot in search of a romantic
end.
I would like to think that I will always have a
friend on Asteroid B-612,
Though he would much rather spend time with
his rosy partner.
I learned a great deal living among small figures
and tall tales,
They have given me hope for something to find,
Though sometimes I wonder if it has only ever
been fiction.
Have I really gone through all of this for the
sake of something that only exists after this life?

Let the night sky be my salvation from the terror
in my heart.
The anxiety that has pushed me forward has
suddenly frozen me in place.
Crystallized and mirrored I will spend myself as
a beacon,

A reflection of the light others bring and an
instrument for ubiquity.
In a meteor storm I imagine myself shattering,
Sending the pieces of myself to be consumed
across galaxies.
I was never meant to stay in one place,
Rather I now see myself belonging within the
hearts of suns;
Made of hydrogen, I will burn.

Sample the stars and you will find me there,
A catalyst fueling the way they shine.
When I have gone, I hope that they will live on
just long enough for someone else to come
along.

Gratitude

For all of the thank-you's that went unsaid,
For the welcomes that were silent,
The graciousness that was not interpreted,
It is not too late.

I have left a lot of appreciation on the table and
in turn have not accepted mine.
There are people who I owe a life-debt to that
have no way to cash in.
After so much time, is it weird to bring up past
mistakes or show love late?
Is it okay to pour my heart out over a casual chat
or should I wait for a more appropriate time?
Though I know that 'time' exists only in the
fictional future and my late night imagination.

I wonder if it would change anything despite its
lateness.
To tell you that I modelled myself in your image,
With so much of me being from you and not
him.
I never have told you how often I have thanked
you in my head,
Regretted things I have said or even just wanted
to hug you.

I recognize how inept I am with sharing how I
value others.
I understand I have not been the most vocal
when it comes time to thank.
I simply hope you understand that words are not
enough for me to let you know,
I am forever grateful for you.

A Letter Left Unread

I hope that one day I'll be able to read aloud the letter I wrote you.
Simply scanning the words or thinking about the contents of the envelope brings tears to my eyes.
To think there was no warning and now I will never again be able to see you in this life,
It feels all too much.
It really makes me wonder about what you would think about my life now.
I have done so much that I wish I could share with you,
So much so that I think I can finally say that I am proud of who I am.
I have become someone that I wish you could meet.

I want you to know that nothing has been the same since you left.
Your life has molded ours, but your loss has separated us.
We do not know how to be together without you,

I suppose it is just something we have to learn
again.
I know it is not what you would have wanted,
nor would be our sadness,
But here I am speaking to the piece of my heart
that holds you… alone in my room.

You sit there frozen in time on my desk, smiling
as if nothing went wrong.
I so wish that I could have been there to see you
when you were growing up.
Did you have someone to look up to, the way we
did you?
When you were older did you ever expect that
you would be so missed?
Did you hear our goodbyes and have you felt our
love since?
Will we meet again?
We are left to wonder.

"We will remember you in the stories you told,
the acts of kindness that were never expected,
and the feelings of love we feel on our good
days."

Away to Boston

I think I will go away to Boston.
Certainly, I have spent too much time in this
place,
With the only thing changing around here being
time.
An uncaring and unmoving town cannot keep
me alive.
It certainly won't leave me fulfilled.

With a whole world out across the city limits,
how can anyone here be content?
I can hear the calls of a hustle and bustle life in
the rains that come in the spring,
It makes me yearn to join the melting pot of
nationals, science, and culture.
I imagine myself finding mentors in cafes before
business meetings and ogling at the architecture.
I would live in an Italianate apartment and study
bioengineering with my new entrepreneurial
friends.
Yet here I am… simply envying the tourists that
come and go as they please.

Here we will be sowing seeds that will root this
summer and bloom in the fall.

My fear is that if I stay one more year in this
place, I myself, will never bloom.
So suffocated by the same ideas and unchanging
routine,
I need to discover what lies beyond the infinite
prairie lands,
And find myself past the rolling hills I have
toiled in for so many years.
…
I must find a way to Boston.

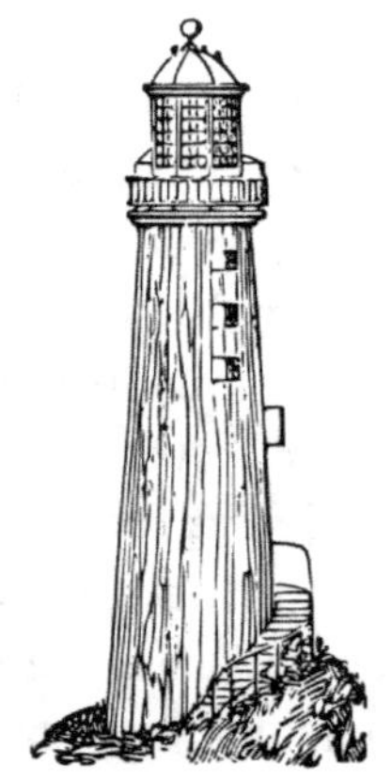

Achievement

I make no special arrangements or celebrations
for my accomplishments or achievements.
There will be no celebration nor extra effort put
into dinner plans.
I am numb to the idea of reaching goals, as my
targets are always moving,
Further and further away they go.
I have lost touch with the idea of discrete wins,
I am tied to a continuous strife to strive for
perfection.

I can be quite contrarian for I wish for
productions from those around me, but neglect
the praise.
My focuses are maintained on reaching higher
and higher,
Increasing the instability of the structure I climb,
I disregard how lofty my ambitions have
become.
Someday I may reach the stars, though I may not
be able to keep my place for long,
Touching the sun has never really been
advisable.

I do wonder how others do it, how they can feel
satisfied stopping.
Is there truly an end to the things you can
achieve?
Why not try for completion, even if impossible?
Why not break the limits and explore the other
side?
Take the impossible as encouraging.
Take it as a challenge and bet your life on it.
Others will tell you that you cannot and will not,
simply because they have not been there
themselves.
So embrace the uncomfortable and risk
everything you hold dear,
Because if you succeed, you have achieved great
things and if you fail…
Well that is an achievement in itself.

Broken Hearts

There are so many stories of lost loves, broken hearts, and forgotten bonds.
They are written and drawn across murals and cities,
In locker notes and on the face of the mirror.
Why do we not fight for the love that was once so familiar?
Are we simply apathetic after the excitement?
Do we not need the trust, love, and respect we knew?
If only one of us could fight for the relationship, maybe things could have been different.

How, after so long, could we burnout and run out of affection?
I wonder if it was me, if it was you… maybe it was me.
I am torn by the feelings I had when you were here and the feelings I have when I see you now.
I feel obligated to say I love you, but I promised I would never lie.
Who is responsible to remind us our place if we no longer share the same sides?
How can I be with you if we don't fit together?

We used to form a tessellation, you were honey
and I was your comb.
My edges have smoothed and yours have only
become rougher,
Now together we only create nonsensical things.

Is it strange for me to wonder now, if we can
save things?
If I were to change and uproot myself for you, I
may resent you.
If you were to move and recreate yourself, I will
undoubtedly be guilt ridden.
Should we leave everything behind and begin
anew,
I will continue to wonder what could have been
without you.
I guess it all comes down to which path I
choose,
Unable to slow down it will be a one way trip,
And so I leave the city.

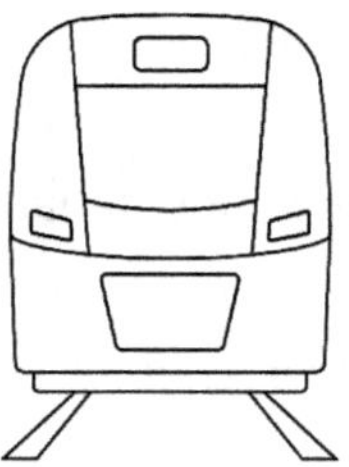

Answering the Question

Philosophical thought is merely a spiral of
reasoning and logical argument,
Occasionally, there is a dash of what we think is
correct in the sense of the universe.
Given structure and experimented on, these
thoughts become science.
Theory then is mere thought until it is found that
we agree, that it is, without a doubt, of some
number of people, a law.
Essentially we are only to know what cannot be
questioned anymore.

Art is a funny thing, for it is the expressiveness
of entropy come together from a lightning storm
of neurological impulses made into reality.
Mathematics deconstructs explanations into a
base form expression that we try to build up new
understanding with, however, in this new
language we find it difficult to translate back
once we have lost ourselves among the
combination of letters and numbers.

Literature and history records all these attempts, though it has been found to be incredibly amnesiac, biased, and in fact plainly incomplete.

So then it seems we are stuck here in what we consider the present, though it has already passed, contemplating whether it is worth our time to ask the question in the first place.
What benefit will we gain from an answer if we are to forget why we asked?
Perhaps we are simply automatons meant to continue our tradition of questioning, hypothesizing, and recording.
So for now in this moment, in previous moments, and in the future, we will forever understand our being to be questioned.

Plot-land

Melancholy gently caresses me with its warm
embrace.
Surrounding the fog of war that are these walls,
The bear traps of placement leave me with
illusionary gifts.
Those around me care more about my location
than my state of being.
Perhaps that's for the best, they simply have
been unable to understand the language I speak.
Though it does make me wonder why they have
chosen to wear pure white,
While they subjugate us to a colorless
uniformity…
If you were to have freedom, might you want to
distinguish your color from ours?

Pensively I sit on the edge of a cliff overlooking
Bear's tidelines,
Thinking upon a time I thought I knew empathy.
Now I only feel the wind on my back that I
actively fight.
Perhaps it would be safer if I was tied to a mast
and sent off to sea,
My crew dying of misfortune and me left to
experience the decay.

One day I will tell my tale in iambic meter for
those to judge,
Hopefully one fair fellow will sit long enough to
be changed by my waves.

Sweet nectar of my Jessamine, we really did
paint the town red.
One last night to haunt my old dwellings before
the past catches up with me.
A wretched spectre briefly making itself
available to the eyes of the public.
As the sun sets on this final day I will find
myself among the skeletons,
And once again the laborers of torment will be
my suitors.
There will be no haste in my step, but I will
ensure my place among the damned.
A man reserved to the land he served, but not to
the mind he has been given.

Mystery House

It was a musty and dull colored place.
Dilapidated and falling apart, this used to be
someone's sanctuary,
Now it has become a spooky outing for
misguided teens in horror movies.
Encumbered by thick fog and an outlier to any
maps, there is sparse life.
The only 'living' things that frequent here are
the ravens and the semi-morphs.
They feast on decay and anything that is
unfortunate enough to find this hidden paradise.

There is a mansion for those brave enough,
which is nothing less than a world of its own.
A place of my own macabre imagination and
distorted brain-scape.
The walls shift faster than sight can see and the
floors double as walls.
Howls in the dark and groans from around
corners vibrate through the hanging skeletons.
The wallpaper is drab, but the portraits are
ornate, colorfully painted and ruined with red.
Halls seem to elongate and close in, twisting
around and around the central red room.

Inside awaits danger, mystery, and well of
course the promise of a wealth of jewels.
You will have to collect yourself and your wits if
you are to brave this bold house.
Beware the roaming spectres, undead horrors,
and undiscovered nightmares.
This is the culmination of centuries of terror.

Stone steps lead up to a wide porch…
I wonder, what will you do?

BLANK

I cannot think.
Rather I cannot control my thoughts or think the
way I know I normally did.
I do feel.
And I feel too much.
It is a silent implosion of a myriad of negative
emotions.
I struggle to identify them and their origins…
I cannot think.
Echoing through my head is trauma and
discourse.
I need to move, to get away from where I am.
Yet it does not help, the problem is not my
surroundings,
It is myself.
I need to get away from the uncomfortableness
of this existence.
The pain of breathing and remembering.
To think that there was a time or will be a time
that I could be caught from this spiral is useless.
I am less than nothing.
I am a burden and I am free of connections with
others.
Maybe I do not believe all of it, yet I still feel
the way I do and need away.

I need help and 80 or more pills will do the trick.
Cutting to ground myself will just ground myself
to the same pain.
The panic attacks were easier, they had an end
point, even if it did feel like death.
I am blind to the source of pain and it feels like
my spirit is trying to fight its way out of my
head.
If I loved you, I am sorry.
If you loved me, I did not know.
This was never selfish.
It was only ever a losing battle.
I fought for as long as I could.
I thought I would be able to win,
But I only delayed the inevitable.
So here I am, pills in hand and a depressant to
wash them down.
One by one, I have the choice to stop, but need
to continue.
They don't all go down smoothly, but it is
something to focus on.
The bottle is empty and soon so will my body.
There will be no letter, no last message, and no
goodbyes.
There will just be my body here.
Someone's lost son, a lost brother, just another
loss to an unrecognized disease.
They will ask themselves what happened and
what they could have done.

Yet they will be left without answers… I simply had none I could give.

I feel the nausea set in and the delusions appear to me.

I feel unwell, though it should be for the last time.

I am sat here keeling over without regret, only the hope for relief.

I think. This is the end.

At last. I wonder what is next.

Status Quorum

Babbling beluga whales atop the Tower of
Babel,
A fever dream in blonde color with sensations of
rainbows,
Insanity merely repeats among the clown
managers.
They don't necessarily have the best planning
schedules…
Their budgets include ear worms and candy
corn.

Who is to say what is proper?
Stuck in a stuffy suit and tie, why not dye that tie
and put it around your arm?
Who needs to have scruff to look gruff when
you can simply ignore complacency?
The buildings downtown have become empty
and the streets are filled with water,
Just another summer disaster for us to celebrate
overcoming.
I look forward to drinking with my late hamsters
and kicking back with Hawking of course.
I will jest till the cows jump the moon, since life
is ridiculous anyway,

Am I really the only one who saw the film about drugs?

…

Or was I on drugs in the film?

Emptying my pockets I realise I forgot to remember you.
I lost my phone somewhere along the line, but it is easily replaceable with a tin can.
Where I am headed my compatriots will surely be impressed.
I do wonder where I am now, between a machine and another machine, at least they have pretty lights.
Polka dotted poker faces will convene around a round table and knight me to their court.
A king of fools and a pauper of diamonds, I will hope for coal on Christmas.
Magically transported to another life of crossing streets and playing violin for myself,
It is tricky finding where to put the string in a hay bale.

I will watch as the microbes bring me to the next stage of my life,
Hopefully it is a more regular one.

…

A feral fungal feline?
I do wonder if this is supposed to be normal.

Circle of Fire

Packaged by bows and swords, I was shielded
by towering walls.
Balls of mystery were given bouncy properties
to entertain.
Crane your head around and you will find me
around the corner.
A loner to the magic, wizards have made for
enchantresses.
Transcendent across the river Styx I have found
home in the marsh.
Harsh is the life of a half-blooded soul warmed
by the fires of hatred and cooled by a chance at
love.
Above the river lies the walls of my prison and
doors to other-worlds, though I am unsure,
which way is the right way down.
Crowned by the opportunity of stability I will
stay my ground on the cliffs of fate.
Dated by carbon you will find complete decay,
unknown is my age or destiny.
Infinitely I will be homebound, yet never quite
reach there.
Bare crow talons will scoop my body from the
giving nest and bring me a new place to roam.

Sewn to the idea of acquiring a new soul to free
myself, I have left my own behind.
Shined through the sun my restoration will come
packaged in a dragon.

For AG-irl

It's in the way you hug me before speaking, so
sweet and impatiently.
Your head tucks into my chest and I can feel the
trust between us.
The way we laugh at each other when we do
something dumb,
Makes me feel comfortable sharing myself with
you.
I have eaten your hair a few times, but I have
gotten used to the taste.

Sarcasm makes up nightly conversation and
makes me sure you don't take yourself too
seriously.
You hate to laugh at my jokes, but I can tell you
enjoy them,
That, along with my ramblings about things I
know you had no interest in before.
It means the world to me that you are curious
about mine,
Though I am certain you see the world in an
entirely different hue,
I find your unending fascinations and facts
endearing.

Whether we are wrapped around each other in a
blanket fort,
Under the stars at night in an open field,
Or exploring a vegetation filled glade,
I am happy to be wherever you are.

Our story is just beginning.
Though we have hardly had time to discover
each other's annoying tendencies,
Things we can't stand,
Or how often we will argue,
I am quite optimistic.

Sit Next to Me

Stumbling backwards onto a bench I maintain
pressure.
I want to stay for long enough to prepare you for
the next chapter,
But it's unclear how much time we have left.
So I will stop my wondering for once and focus
on this moment with you.
I will stay calm for the both of us, as you
struggle to understand what happened.

Sit next to me and listen to my heart beat.
Listen to how it stays in rhythm with yours.
When it stops, know that I was glad you were
beside me.
My body will be left behind as a reminder that I
was there,
But you must go on without it.
This moment will stay with you and it will haunt
your nightmares,
Maybe for weeks, months, even years,
But you will overcome it.
You do not need to say goodbye, though you
will need to move on.
We were lucky to spend every second we did on
each other,

Though there was simply not enough to get us
both by,
I wish for you to lead the life I always knew you
could,
Just now without me.

Remember the life and fun, but don't forget the
things we have overcome.
Remember the tears left on my sweatshirt, but
keep in mind the lessons we learned.
I am starting to sound more and more poetic, but
how else can I get out all of what I want to say
before I go.
I always thought there would be more time to
tell you how much I have appreciated you,
And how I wanted all of the ups and downs to
continue…

Whisked away by a calm breeze,
I will fall away.

Wake

I spend my time in the writing room,
An inescapable prison below this House of
Dreams.
Where there was once, and will again, be a battle
of light and dark.
It is impossible to tell how much time has
passed, but I will write of my Return.
Surrounded only by the serene ocean green and
white noise of the water around me,
I am threatened by blotted silhouettes and a
mirror of misrepresentation.
A decade in the making I will escape from the
shackles of this desk and ink my last line,
This typewriter will no longer chain me to a
promise of eternity.

I will write my way through twisted portraits
and painted terror,
Across the infinite expanse of an altered world,
I must find my way back to the port of this lake.
Reality has been stained with thermos rings from
caffeine leaks,
But I will shine my flashlight through to cut the
darkness away.

The unrecognizable muse has been saved, yet
we are still besieged by the old Gods.
If we are to slay this demon, like the lighthouse
diver I must find balance.

Extraordinary events will continue to wreak
havoc and break our laws of quantum physics.
Objects of immense paranatural power will
create waves of madness,
But we will make our way through the Ashtray
maze to take control the course of time.
So join together in my dark disquiet as we head
to war.
We do not yet know the face of evil, but we will
fight to remedy the storm.

Poetry, Part II

Poetry is not always written for others,
Not always for ourselves,
Not even for those dedicated.
Sometimes poems are written and burned for the
sake of releasing them from their cages.

A lot of poems are made from the feelings and
memories we have,
A lot from stolen moments and treasured pain,
Even a number from the dreams we dare to
remember.
Though sometimes poetry is simply words on a
page, written as a reminder.

We share poetry sometimes as a shy attempt at
sharing our private selves,
Or an invitation for analysis.
Yet oftentimes our poems are read in reflection
of the audience's life and not our own.
We yearn for understanding, yet find only false
relatability.

Poems can be structured or loose, nice or
disruptive, long or short, even silly or serious.

Sometimes they can meld into one another, but
how much weight are these styles given?
I wonder if the reader ever interprets my poetry
the way I meant to write it.
Have I opened a door that leads away from me
or were the words I used mistranslated?
Perhaps I simply do not have what it takes to
write true poetry, though who is it that can
define me or my loosely structured, nicely
written, disruptions that I write seriously silly?
I suppose as soon as the author walks away from
their work, they are already dead.

When we read poetry, we are fixed to our own
past and environment,
Changing how we consume and experience the
poetry we read,
Yet we are also drawn to find ourselves among
the words alongside the poet.
Perhaps we are all nothing more than characters
in search of an author that has already left.